TABLE OF CONTENTS

W9-ATC-551

Write the first letter of each picture's name.
Read the animal names.
Write the problem numbers in the circles by the correct animals.

_____ _____ _____

_____

1. _____ _____ _____

_____ _____ _____

_____

2. _____ _____ _____

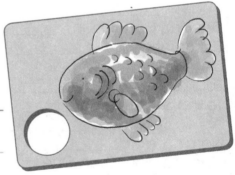

_____ _____ _____ _____

_____

3. _____ _____ _____ _____

_____ _____ _____ _____

_____

4. _____ _____ _____

Circle the pictures that have the **short a** sound.

short a sound
hat

1.

2.

3.
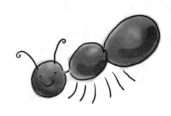   

4.
  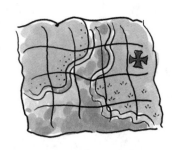 

Circle the pictures that have the **short e** sound.

1.

2.

3.

4.

SHORT I

Circle the pictures that have the **short i** sound.

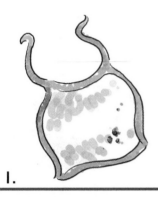

1.

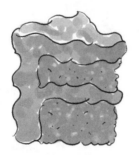

2.

3.

4.

Circle the pictures that have the **short o** sound.

short o sound
clock

1.

2.

3.

4.

SHORT U

Circle the pictures that have the **short u** sound.

1.

2.

3.

4.

The letters **a**, **e**, **i**, **o**, and **u** are **vowels**.
These words have **short vowel** sounds:

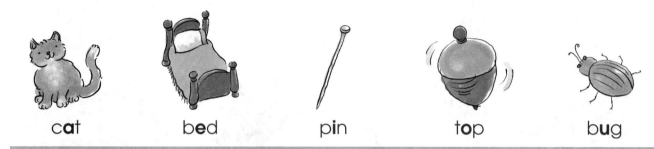

cat   bed   pin   top   bug

Look at the pictures. Say the words.
Write the short vowels in the puzzle.

ACROSS

2.

3.

5.

DOWN

1.

2.

4.

1.h			2.s		c	k
3.t	4.	n				
	g					
5.p	g					

Write short vowels to complete the words.

a e i o u
fox

1. t__n

2. __c__t

3. p__g

4. b__s

5. d__ll

6. f__n

7. f__sh

8. __n__st

9. d__ck

Write the **long a** words to answer the riddles.

long **a** sound
snake

rain	gray	cake
day	gate	snail

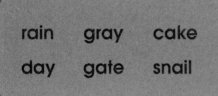

1. I live in a shell.

_____

_ _ _ _ _ _ _ _ _ _ _ _ _ _

_____

2. I wear candles on your birthday.

_____

_ _ _ _ _ _ _ _ _ _ _ _ _ _

_____

3. I make flowers grow.

_____

_ _ _ _ _ _ _ _ _ _ _ _ _ _

_____

4. I am the opposite of night.

_____

_ _ _ _ _ _ _ _ _ _ _ _ _ _

_____

5. Write two **long a** words that begin with **g**.

_____   _____

_ _ _ _ _ _ _ _ _ _ _ _   _ _ _ _ _ _ _ _ _ _ _ _

_____   _____

LONG E

Write the **long e** words to answer the riddles.

long e sound
seal

| sheep | leaf | he |
| three | tree | me |

1. I come after two.

_____

_ _ _ _ _ _ _ _ _ _ _ _

_____

2. I grow outside.

_____

_ _ _ _ _ _ _ _ _ _ _ _

_____

3. I say "baa!"

_____

_ _ _ _ _ _ _ _ _ _ _ _

_____

4. I grow on a tree.

_____

_ _ _ _ _ _ _ _ _ _ _ _

_____

5. Write two two-letter **long e** words.

_____   _____

_ _ _ _ _ _ _ _ _ _   _ _ _ _ _ _ _ _ _ _

_____   _____

Write the **long i** words to answer the riddles.

long i sound
kite

fly	right	tie
bike	tight	nine

1. You can ride me.

_____
_____
_____

2. I come before ten.

_____
_____
_____

3. A plane can do this.

_____
_____
_____

4. This is the opposite of left.

_____
_____

5. Write two **long i** words that begin with **t**.

_____   _____

_____   _____

_____   _____

Write the **long o** words to answer the riddles.

rose	goat	rope
nose	boat	note

1. I live on a farm.

_____

2. You can tie things
   with me.

_____

3. I move in water.

_____

4. I am a kind of
   flower.

_____

5. Write two **long o** words that begin with **n**.

_____   _____

_____   _____

LONG U

Write the **long u** words to answer the riddles.

long **u** sound **cube**

| cute | tube | new |
| huge | few | glue |

1. Toothpaste comes in a _____ .

2. Use me to stick
   things together. _____

3. A whale is _____ .

4. Babies are _____ .

5. Write two **long u** words that end with **ew**.

_____ _____

_____ _____

LONG VOWEL PUZZLE

As you've learned, the letters **a**, **e**, **i**, **o**, and **u** are **vowels**.
A **long vowel** says its own name.
These words have **long vowel** sounds:

c**a**ke   tr**ee**   h**i**ve   r**o**pe   m**u**le

Look at the pictures. Say the words.
Write the long vowels in the puzzle.

ACROSS

1.
4.
6.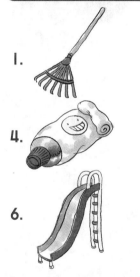

DOWN

2.
3.
5.

Puzzle grid:

1. r _ | 2. k e | 3. b
4. t _ | 5. b e
e |
| n
6. s l _ d e

Draw lines from the pictures to the long vowel sounds heard in their names.

long a

long e

long i

long o

long u

PREDICTING OUTCOMES

Check what will happen next.

1. The sun gets hot.

2. It is time to play.

3. Let's cool off!

4. It is time for lunch.

ORDINAL NUMBERS

An **ordinal number** tells the position of an object.

first   second   third   fourth   fifth

Write the places of the cars.

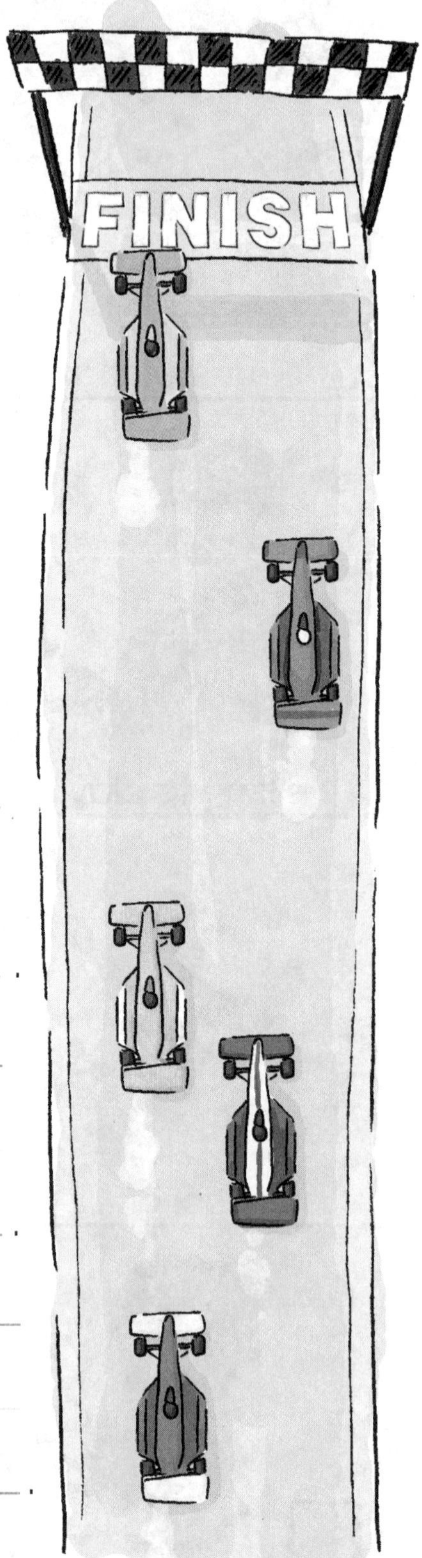

_____

1. The **red** car is _____ .

_____

2. The **blue** car is _____ .

_____

3. The **green** car is _____ .

_____

4. The **yellow** car is _____ .

_____

5. The **orange** car is _____ .

Can you tell the difference between living and non-living things?
Write the words from the box on the correct lists.

dog	ball	top
bird	goat	doll

Living	Non-living
_____	_____
_____	_____
_____	_____
_____	_____
_____	_____
_____	_____
_____	_____

STORY ORDER

It is fun to make a costume.
From 1–6, number the pictures in order.

PREDICTING OUTCOMES

Check what will happen next.

1.

2.

Circle the correct answers.

1. The magician is wearing a tall hat.

   yes   **no**

2. He is wearing a purple cape.

   yes   **no**

3. He has a magic wand.

   yes   **no**

4. He is wearing a red tie.

   yes   **no**

5. He has little shoes.

   yes   **no**

6. There is a rabbit in his hat.

   yes   **no**

STORY ORDER

Write 1 by what happens first.
Write 2 by what happens next.
Write 3 by what happens last.

1.

_____ _____ _____

2.

_____ _____ _____

The amusement park opens today!
From 1–6, number the names in alphabetical order.

FERRIS WHEEL

ROLLER COASTER

BUMPER CARS

LOG RIDE

CAROUSEL

WAVE POOL

Which is your favorite ride?

_____

_____

_____

Cross out the things you **do not** need.

1. To feed your dog, you need:

a dish   food   a collar

2. To wash your bike, you need:

soap   water   gloves

3. To write a story, you need:

  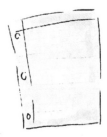

a book   a pencil   paper

4. To send a letter, you need:

a stamp   a car   an envelope

OPPOSITES

Write the correct words to finish the sentences.

hot	open	old
closed	cold	new

1. Ben just got a bike.
   The bike is _____.

   _____

   _____

2. No one is in the school.
   The school is _____.

   _____

   _____

3. Dad lit the grill.
   The grill is _____.

   _____

   _____

4. Mother went in the store.
   The store is _____.

   _____

   _____

5. Lily had the toy years ago.
   The toy is _____.

   _____

   _____

6. It is snowing again.
   It is _____.

   _____

   _____

1. Circle three things we eat.
   Draw a line under a pet.

2. Circle three pictures that rhyme.
   Draw a line under a number.

3. Circle three things that fly.
   Draw a line under a toy.

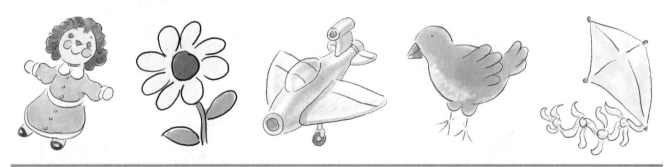

4. Circle three farm animals.
   Draw a line under a zoo animal.

DRAWING CONCLUSIONS

Read the clues.
Write the names under the correct pictures.

1. Jill plays the violin.
2. Zeke plays baseball.
3. Anna likes to swim.
4. Pedro plays soccer.
5. Adam makes things.

_____

_____

_____

_____

_____

Read the clues.
Write the names under the correct pictures.

1. Sue likes to wear flip-flops.
2. Eddie always wears a cap.
3. Rachel has long hair.
4. Peter wears glasses.
5. Beth has a backpack.

Read the story.

Side by side,
Mother and I glide.
Not too fast or too slow,
Through the water we go.

We went past Mr. Frog,
Who is sitting on a log.
We went past Mrs. Mink,
Who had come for a drink.
We went past Miss Otter,
Who is playing in the water.
We went past Mr. Fox,
Who waved from a rock.

Side by side,
Mother and I glide.

Check the correct answers.

1. Who came for a drink?    ☐   ☐

2. Who sat on a log?   ☐   ☐

3. Who waved from a rock?   ☐   ☐

4. Who is playing in the water?    ☐   ☐

A zoo has many helpers to take care of the animals.
Read the clues.
Write the names under the correct pictures.

1. Henry keeps the animals' homes clean.
2. Liz helps sick animals.
3. Chan works with the sea animals.
4. Stacy feeds hungry animals.

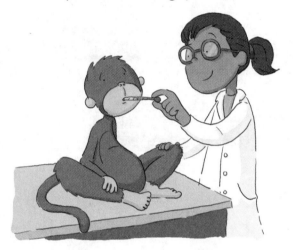

_____

_____

_____

_____

_____

_____

_____

_____

LOGICAL REASONING

Read the clues. Mark the chart with checks.
The first one is done for you.

1. Everyone had fruit.

2. Dad and Jake had a taco.

3. Mom had a salad.

4. Ashley had a turkey sandwich.

5. Mom, Jake, and Ashley had juice.

6. Dad had milk.

	milk	juice	fruit	salad	taco	sandwich
Dad			✔			
Jake			✔			
Mom			✔			
Ashley			✔			

Write the names under the correct meals.

_____

_____

_____

_____

_____

_____

_____

_____

A **telling sentence** begins with a capital letter.
It ends with a period (.).

Use the ☰ to show where capital letters go.
Then put periods (.) at the end of the sentences.
The first one is done for you.

1. o͟u͟r dog is hungry.

2. dad brings food

3. skip eats quickly

4. food goes on the floor

5. dogs are messy

6. now I need to clean up

7. Write a telling sentence.

_____

_____

_____

_____

ASKING SENTENCES

An **asking sentence** asks about something or someone.
It ends with a question mark (**?**).

Use the ☰ to show where capital letters go. Then put question marks (**?**) at the end of the sentences that ask questions and a period (**.**) at the end of the telling sentence. The first one is done for you.

1. <u>i</u>s Mother home**?**

2. where did she go

3. when will she be back

4. who baked the cookies

5. they are good

6. may I have another one

7. Write an asking sentence.

_____

NAMING WORDS

Some **naming words** name people or animals.

Here are a few examples:
girl   brother   cat   horse

Read the sentences. Write the naming words that name people or animals.
The first one is done for you.

1. Dad drove away. _____

2. The farmer waved. _____

3. The cows were eating. _____

4. Our dog barked. _____

5. A chicken ran away. _____

Some **naming words** name places or things.

Here are a few examples:
school   city   shoe   apple

```
zoo   house   pizza
book   town   bike
```

Which words name places, and which words name things?
Write the words from the box on the correct lists.

Places	**Things**

_____ | _____

_____ | _____

_____ | _____

Write a naming word for a place and a naming word for a thing.

Place	**Thing**

_____ | _____

NAMING MORE THAN ONE

Many words add **s** to name **more than one**.

Here are a few examples:
hens   **frogs**   **rings**

dog   spot   cat

bone   ear

Add **s** to the naming words from the box to finish the sentences.
The first one is done for you.

1. Jamie has two  .

2. One dog has brown _____ .

3. One dog has black _____ .

4. They run after _____ .

5. They bury _____ .

An **action word** tells what someone or something does.

Here are a few examples:

    jump   **cry**   **eat**   **push**

Read the sentences. Write the action words.
The first one is done for you.

1. Let's play ball. _____ play _____

2. Jake hits the ball. _____

3. The ball flies high. _____

4. Megan runs after it. _____

5. Will she catch it? _____

plant   eat   water
pull   grow

Add **s** to the action words from the box to finish the sentences.
The first one is done for you.

1. Each spring, Bob  plants a garden.

2. He _____ pretty flowers.

3. Dad _____ weeds.

4. Anna _____ the garden.

5. Sometimes a rabbit _____ the flowers.

DESCRIBING WORDS

Some **describing words** tell how things sound or feel.

Here are a few examples:
quiet   warm   smooth

hot   cold   loud
wet   soft

Write the describing words from the box to finish the sentences.
The first one is done for you.

1. The sun is  .

2. A jet makes a _____ sound.

3. Ice cream is _____ .

4. The kitten has _____ fur.

5. Don't slip on the _____ grass.

DESCRIBING WORDS

Some **describing words** tell size, color, or amount.

Here are a few examples:
    small   **red**   **seven**

Underline the describing words in the sentences.
The first one is done for you.

1. Lady is a <u>big</u> cat.

2. She had three kittens.

3. Tiger is the striped kitten.

4. Jet is the black kitten.

5. The little kitten is Socks.

6. We now have four cats.

7. Write a sentence using a describing word.
   Underline the describing word.

_____

- -

_____

_____

- -

_____

CONTRACTIONS

A **contraction** is a short way to write two words.

I am → I'm

haven't   don't   Let's
aren't   won't

Write the contractions for the underlined words.
The first one is done for you.

1. Please <u>do not</u> go. _____don't_____

2. We <u>are not</u> done. _____

3. We <u>have not</u> painted it. _____

4. <u>Let us</u> paint it red. _____

5. It <u>will not</u> take long. _____

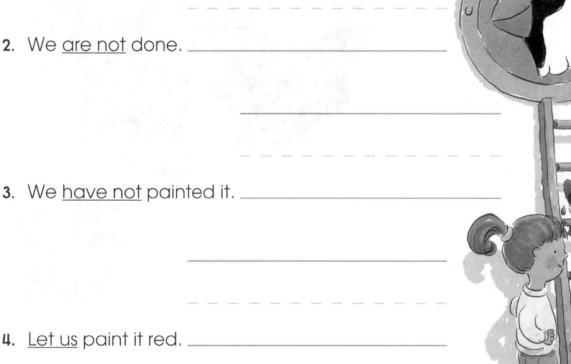

ADDITION

$2 + 1 = \underline{\ 3\ }$ $3 + 2 = \underline{\ 5\ }$

Add.

 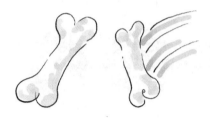

1. $3 + 1 = \underline{\ \ \ \ }$ 2. $1 + 1 = \underline{\ \ \ \ }$

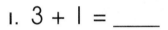

  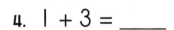

3. $2 + 2 = \underline{\ \ \ \ }$ 4. $1 + 3 = \underline{\ \ \ \ }$

5. $3 + 2 = \underline{\ \ \ \ }$ 6. $2 + 1 = \underline{\ \ \ \ }$

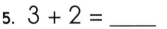 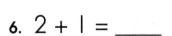

SUBTRACTION

$4 - 1 = \underline{\ 3\ }$

$5 - 2 = \underline{\ 3\ }$

Subtract. Cross out pictures to show the equations.
Write how many are left.

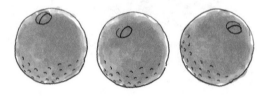

1. $3 - 1 = \underline{\qquad}$

2. $4 - 2 = \underline{\qquad}$

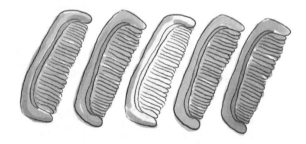

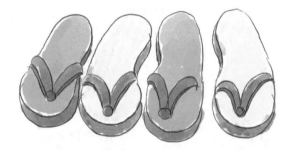

3. $5 - 2 = \underline{\qquad}$

4. $4 - 3 = \underline{\qquad}$

5. $3 - 2 = \underline{\qquad}$

6. $5 - 3 = \underline{\qquad}$

ADDITION

 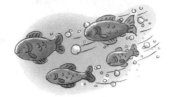

$3 + 4 = \underline{\;7\;}$

$2 + 0 = \underline{\;2\;}$

Add.

1. $0 + 5 = \underline{\quad}$

2. $3 + 2 = \underline{\quad}$

3. $7 + 1 = \underline{\quad}$

4. $4 + 3 = \underline{\quad}$

5. $5 + 3 = \underline{\quad}$

6. $5 + 2 = \underline{\quad}$

7. $1 + 6 = \underline{\quad}$

8. $8 + 0 = \underline{\quad}$

9. $3 + 5 = \underline{\quad}$

10. $4 + 1 = \underline{\quad}$

11. $2 + 2 = \underline{\quad}$

12. $1 + 3 = \underline{\quad}$

SUBTRACTION

5 − 3 = __2__

3 − 0 = __3__

Subtract.

1. 4 − 3 = ____

2. 8 − 4 = ____

3. 6 − 4 = ____

4. 6 − 5 = ____

5. 5 − 1 = ____

6. 8 − 6 = ____

7. 7 − 0 = ____

8. 3 − 2 = ____

9. 7 − 5 = ____

10. 6 − 6 = ____

11. 7 − 1 = ____

12. 6 − 2 = ____

The answer to an addition problem is called the **sum**.
The answer to a subtraction problem is called the **difference**.

Add to find the sums.

| 1. | 4
+ 3 | 2. | 2
+ 6 | 3. | 1
+ 7 | 4. | 2
+ 4 |

| 5. | 5
+ 2 | 6. | 5
+ 3 | 7. | 6
+ 1 | 8. | 3
+ 3 |

Subtract to find the differences.

| 9. | 6
− 5 | 10. | 8
− 8 | 11. | 8
− 2 | 12. | 4
− 2 |

| 13. | 6
− 3 | 14. | 8
− 6 | 15. | 7
− 5 | 16. | 7
− 4 |

Counting on helps you find the sum.
To count on, start with the greater number.
Count 3 more numbers than 5. The sum is 8.

$$\begin{array}{r} 5 \\ +\ 3 \\ \hline 8 \end{array}$$

6, 7, 8

0 1 2 3 4 5 6 7 8 9 10 11 12

Count on to find the sums.

1. $4 + 8 =$ _____

2. $7 + 4 =$ _____

3. $6 + 6 =$ _____

4. $5 + 5 =$ _____

5. $11 + 1 =$ _____

6. $9 + 3 =$ _____

7. $\begin{array}{r} 5 \\ +\ 4 \\ \hline \end{array}$

8. $\begin{array}{r} 10 \\ +\ 2 \\ \hline \end{array}$

9. $\begin{array}{r} 3 \\ +\ 7 \\ \hline \end{array}$

10. $\begin{array}{r} 8 \\ +\ 1 \\ \hline \end{array}$

11. $\begin{array}{r} 4 \\ +\ 6 \\ \hline \end{array}$

12. $\begin{array}{r} 5 \\ +\ 6 \\ \hline \end{array}$

13. $\begin{array}{r} 9 \\ +\ 2 \\ \hline \end{array}$

14. $\begin{array}{r} 7 \\ +\ 5 \\ \hline \end{array}$

COUNTING BACK

Counting back helps you find the difference.
To count back, start with the greater number.
Count 5 numbers back from 11. The difference is 6.

$$11 - 5 = 6$$

10, 9, 8, 7, 6

0 1 2 3 4 5 6 7 8 9 10 11 12

Count back to find the differences.

1. $11 - 4 =$ _____

2. $12 - 5 =$ _____

3. $11 - 2 =$ _____

4. $12 - 7 =$ _____

5. $9 - 3 =$ _____

6. $10 - 6 =$ _____

7. $\begin{array}{r} 12 \\ -\ 4 \\ \hline \end{array}$

8. $\begin{array}{r} 11 \\ -\ 6 \\ \hline \end{array}$

9. $\begin{array}{r} 11 \\ -\ 7 \\ \hline \end{array}$

10. $\begin{array}{r} 12 \\ -\ 8 \\ \hline \end{array}$

11. $\begin{array}{r} 10 \\ -\ 2 \\ \hline \end{array}$

12. $\begin{array}{r} 11 \\ -\ 5 \\ \hline \end{array}$

13. $\begin{array}{r} 12 \\ -\ 6 \\ \hline \end{array}$

14. $\begin{array}{r} 12 \\ -\ 3 \\ \hline \end{array}$

Counting Back

ADDITION USING A NUMBER LINE

A number line can help you find a sum.
Count 2 more than 5.

$$\begin{array}{r} 5 \\ + \ 2 \\ \hline 7 \end{array}$$

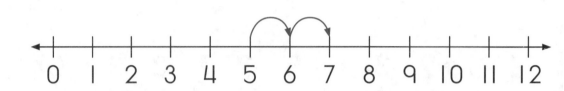

Use the number line to find the sums.

1. $\begin{array}{r} 7 \\ + \ 2 \\ \hline \end{array}$
  2. $\begin{array}{r} 5 \\ + \ 5 \\ \hline \end{array}$
  3. $\begin{array}{r} 4 \\ + \ 4 \\ \hline \end{array}$
  4. $\begin{array}{r} 7 \\ + \ 4 \\ \hline \end{array}$

5. $\begin{array}{r} 8 \\ + \ 4 \\ \hline \end{array}$
  6. $\begin{array}{r} 9 \\ + \ 2 \\ \hline \end{array}$
  7. $\begin{array}{r} 4 \\ + \ 3 \\ \hline \end{array}$
  8. $\begin{array}{r} 6 \\ + \ 2 \\ \hline \end{array}$

9. $\begin{array}{r} 7 \\ + \ 5 \\ \hline \end{array}$
  10. $\begin{array}{r} 6 \\ + \ 3 \\ \hline \end{array}$
  11. $\begin{array}{r} 8 \\ + \ 2 \\ \hline \end{array}$
  12. $\begin{array}{r} 9 \\ + \ 3 \\ \hline \end{array}$

13. $\begin{array}{r} 5 \\ + \ 3 \\ \hline \end{array}$
  14. $\begin{array}{r} 4 \\ + \ 5 \\ \hline \end{array}$
  15. $\begin{array}{r} 6 \\ + \ 4 \\ \hline \end{array}$
  16. $\begin{array}{r} 3 \\ + \ 8 \\ \hline \end{array}$

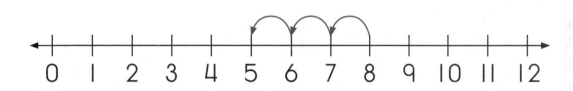

A number line can help you find a difference.
Count 3 less than 8.

```
  8
- 3
-----
  5
```

0 1 2 3 4 5 6 7 8 9 10 11 12

Use the number line to find the differences.

1. $\begin{array}{r} 11 \\ -\ 4 \\ \hline \end{array}$
2. $\begin{array}{r} 12 \\ -\ 7 \\ \hline \end{array}$
3. $\begin{array}{r} 8 \\ -\ 3 \\ \hline \end{array}$
4. $\begin{array}{r} 9 \\ -\ 5 \\ \hline \end{array}$

5. $\begin{array}{r} 7 \\ -\ 4 \\ \hline \end{array}$
6. $\begin{array}{r} 9 \\ -\ 4 \\ \hline \end{array}$
7. $\begin{array}{r} 10 \\ -\ 2 \\ \hline \end{array}$
8. $\begin{array}{r} 8 \\ -\ 5 \\ \hline \end{array}$

9. $\begin{array}{r} 9 \\ -\ 6 \\ \hline \end{array}$
10. $\begin{array}{r} 6 \\ -\ 5 \\ \hline \end{array}$
11. $\begin{array}{r} 12 \\ -\ 5 \\ \hline \end{array}$
12. $\begin{array}{r} 10 \\ -\ 4 \\ \hline \end{array}$

13. $\begin{array}{r} 12 \\ -\ 8 \\ \hline \end{array}$
14. $\begin{array}{r} 11 \\ -\ 2 \\ \hline \end{array}$
15. $\begin{array}{r} 9 \\ -\ 8 \\ \hline \end{array}$
16. $\begin{array}{r} 11 \\ -\ 6 \\ \hline \end{array}$

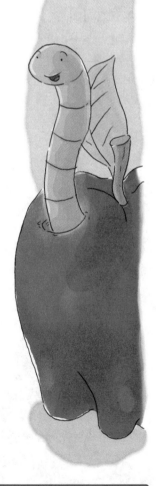

Add and subtract to find the sums and differences.

1. 8
    − 3
    ___

2. 11
    − 3
    ___

3. 9
    + 2
    ___

4. 10
    − 4
    ___

5. 6
    + 3
    ___

6. 12
    − 3
    ___

7. 6
    + 4
    ___

8. 7
    + 5
    ___

9. 11
    − 5
    ___

10. 9
    − 6
    ___

11. 5
    + 5
    ___

12. 12
    − 7
    ___

13. 8
    + 2
    ___

14. 10
    − 5
    ___

15. 9
    + 3
    ___

16. 12
    − 5
    ___

Write + and − to make the number sentences true.
The first one is done for you.

1. $9 \boxed{-} 5 = 4$

2. $10 \boxed{} 4 = 6$

3. $6 \boxed{} 6 = 12$

4. $6 \boxed{} 2 = 4$

5. $8 \boxed{} 4 = 12$

6. $7 \boxed{} 4 = 3$

7. $6 \boxed{} 4 = 2$

8. $5 \boxed{} 5 = 10$

9. $4 \boxed{} 6 = 10$

10. $12 \boxed{} 5 = 7$

11. $8 \boxed{} 2 = 10$

12. $11 \boxed{} 9 = 2$

13. $5 \boxed{} 6 = 11$

14. $8 \boxed{} 5 = 3$

15. $6 \boxed{} 3 = 9$

Find the sums and differences.
Circle the bear with the greatest answer.

Greatest means largest or biggest.

10	0	8	12	4	9
− 2	+ 8	+ 1	− 7	+ 1	− 3
+ 4	− 3	+ 2	+ 6	− 0	+ 5
− 5	+ 7	− 4	− 1	+ 6	− 3
=	=	=	=	=	=

Circle the equations that make the sums.

1. **10**

$7 + 3$

$8 + 1$

$5 + 5$

$6 + 4$

2. **11**

$9 + 2$

$6 + 5$

$8 + 4$

$3 + 8$

3. **12**

$4 + 8$

$9 + 3$

$5 + 7$

$6 + 6$

4. **13**

$5 + 7$

$8 + 5$

$10 + 3$

$9 + 4$

5. **14**

$4 + 10$

$7 + 7$

$6 + 8$

$5 + 9$

6. **15**

$10 + 5$

$11 + 3$

$8 + 7$

$9 + 6$

7. **16**

$8 + 8$

$7 + 9$

$6 + 10$

$12 + 5$

8. **17**

$6 + 11$

$10 + 7$

$9 + 8$

$7 + 9$

9. **18**

$12 + 6$

$7 + 11$

$10 + 8$

$9 + 9$

Circle the equations that make the differences.

1.
10
12 − 2

15 − 6

14 − 4

13 − 3

2.
11
13 − 2

11 − 0

12 − 1

15 − 4

3.
12
14 − 2

16 − 4

17 − 4

15 − 3

4.
13
17 − 4

15 − 2

14 − 1

18 − 4

5.
14
12 − 2

18 − 4

16 − 2

17 − 3

6.
15
18 − 3

16 − 1

17 − 2

12 − 3

7.
16
16 − 0

15 − 1

18 − 2

17 − 1

8.
17
15 − 2

18 − 1

16 − 1

17 − 0

9.
18
17 − 1

18 − 0

16 − 2

15 − 3

Find the sums and differences.
Circle the fish with the greatest answer.

8	16	4	9	5	17
+ 4	− 8	+10	+ 8	+ 4	− 5
+ 6	− 7	+ 2	− 5	+ 6	− 1
− 1	+ 3	− 3	+ 6	− 7	+ 5
=	=	=	=	=	=

PLANE FIGURES

Draw lines from the objects to the matching figures.
The first one is done for you.

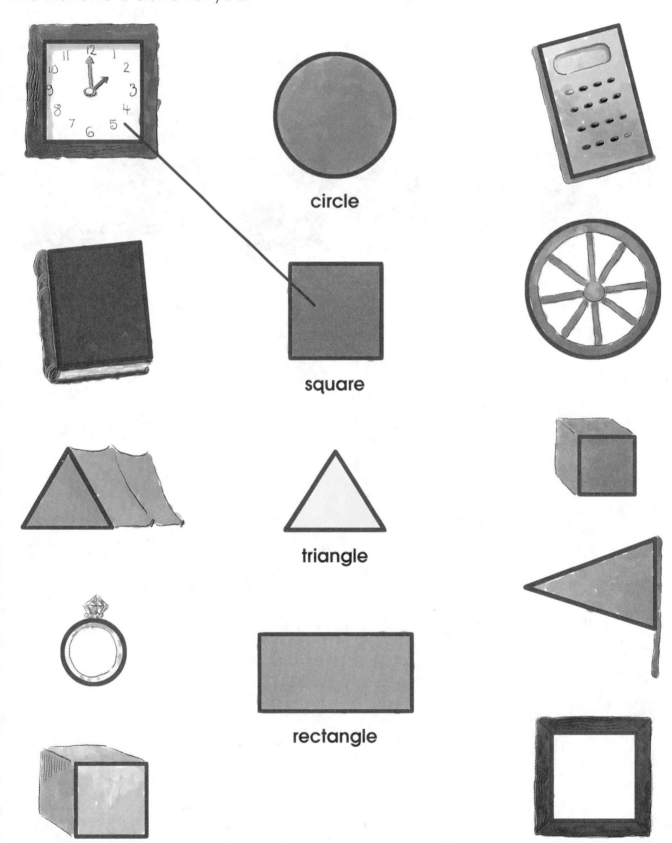

circle

square

triangle

rectangle

SPACE FIGURES

Draw lines from the objects to the matching figures.
The first one is done for you.

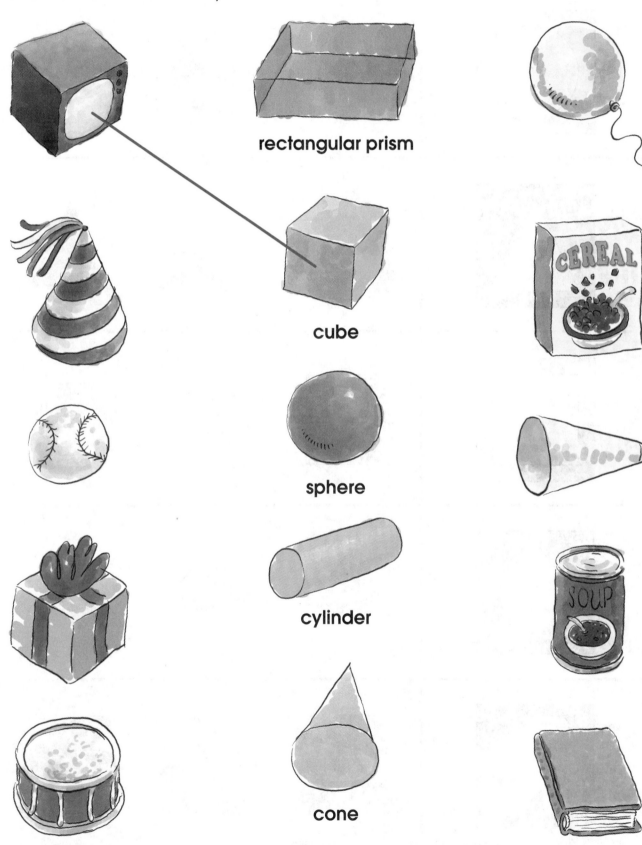

rectangular prism

cube

sphere

cylinder

cone

Circle the shapes that fit the outlines.

1.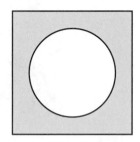

2.

3.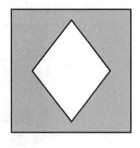

4.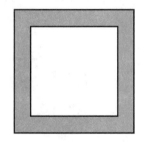

5.

COUNTING BY TENS

How many are there? Write the numbers.
The first one is done for you.

1.   <u> 1 </u> ten <u> 10 </u>
ten

2.   _____ tens _____
twenty

3.   _____ tens _____
thirty

4.   _____ tens _____
forty

5.   _____ tens _____
fifty

6.   _____ tens _____
sixty

7. 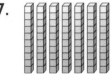 _____ tens _____
seventy

8. 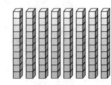 _____ tens _____
eighty

9. 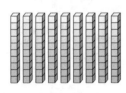 _____ tens _____
ninety

Write the missing numbers.

10. 10 20 ____ 40 50 ____ 70 80 90 100

11. 10 ____ ____ 40 ____ 60 70 ____ 90 ____

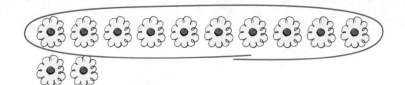

___1___ ten ___2___ ones How many ? ___12___

Circle groups of ten. Write the number of tens and ones.
Then write how many there are in all.

1. _____ ten _____ ones

How many ? _____

2. _____ tens _____ ones

How many ? _____

3. _____ tens _____ ones

How many ☆? _____

4. _____ tens _____ ones

How many 🔔? _____

5. _____ ten _____ ones

How many ? _____

6. _____ ten _____ ones

How many 🎵? _____

Read the numbers.
Write how many tens and how many ones there are.
The first one is done for you.

	tens	ones
1. 65	6	5

	tens	ones
2. 28	___	___

	tens	ones
3. 54	___	___

	tens	ones
4. 66	___	___

	tens	ones
5. 40	___	___

	tens	ones
6. 34	___	___

	tens	ones
7. 81	___	___

	ten	ones
8. 17	___	___

	tens	ones
9. 30	___	___

	tens	ones
10. 71	___	___

	ten	ones
11. 19	___	___

	tens	ones
12. 25	___	___

GREATER THAN AND LESS THAN

Greater means more than.
Less means not as many.

Circle the numbers that are greater.
The first one is done for you.

1. 13 (31)   2. 35 27   3. 50 48

4. 43 34   5. 10 15   6. 25 31

7. 18 10   8. 21 19   9. 23 14

Circle the numbers that are less.
The first one is done for you.

10. (44) 54   11. 18 13   12. 81 18

13. 78 82   14. 25 31   15. 23 36

16. 20 30   17. 62 59   18. 55 48

BEFORE, BETWEEN, AND AFTER

Write the numbers that come **before**.

1. ____ 45
2. ____ 27
3. ____ 24
4. ____ 33

5. ____ 81
6. ____ 30
7. ____ 18
8. ____ 67

Write the numbers that come **between**.

9. 91 ____ 93
10. 53 ____ 55
11. 40 ____ 42

12. 24 ____ 26
13. 17 ____ 19
14. 36 ____ 38

Write the numbers that come **after**.

15. 6 ____
16. 47 ____
17. 25 ____
18. 19 ____

19. 92 ____
20. 50 ____
21. 74 ____
22. 11 ____

PENNIES, NICKELS, AND DIMES

front   back
penny = 1¢

1¢   2¢   3¢   4¢

To count pennies, count by ones.

front   back
nickel = 5¢

5¢   10¢   15¢   20¢

To count nickels, count by fives.

front   back
dime = 10¢

10¢   20¢   30¢   40¢

To count dimes, count by tens.

Count the coins. Write the totals.

1.   _____¢

2.    _____¢

3.   _____¢

PENNIES, NICKELS, AND DIMES

Count by tens, then by fives and ones.

<u>10¢</u> <u>20¢</u> <u>30¢</u> <u>35¢</u> <u>40¢</u> <u>41¢</u> <u>42¢</u> <u> 42 </u>¢

Count on to find the total amounts.
Write the amounts.

1.

___ ___ ___ ___ ___ ___ _____ ¢

2.

___ ___ ___ ___ ___ ___ _____ ¢

3.

___ ___ ___ ___ ___ ___ _____ ¢

4.

___ ___ ___ ___ ___ _____ ¢

PENNIES, NICKELS, AND DIMES

How much do the toys cost?
Count on to find the total amounts.
Write the totals on the price tags.

1.

____ ____ ____ ____ ____ ____

2.

____ ____ ____ ____ ____ ____

3.

____ ____ ____ ____ ____ ____

4.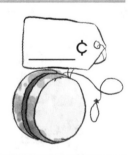

____ ____ ____ ____ ____ ____

5.

____ ____ ____ ____ ____ ____

PENNIES, NICKELS, AND DIMES

Count the coins.
Write the amounts.

1.

_____ ¢

2.

_____ ¢

3.

_____ ¢

4.

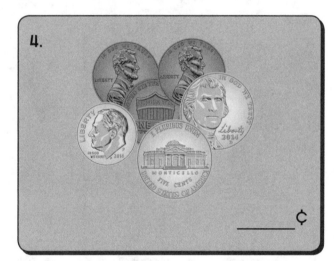

_____ ¢

5.

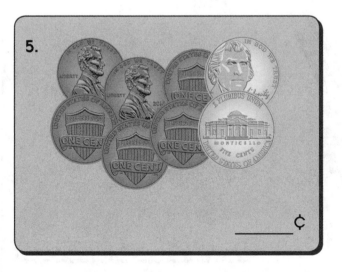

_____ ¢

6.

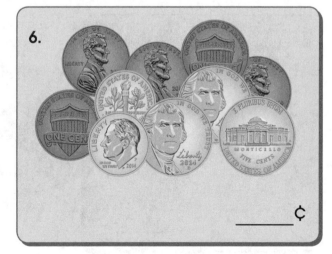

_____ ¢

PENNIES, NICKELS, AND DIMES

Count the coins. Write the amounts.
Then draw lines from the amounts to the art supplies with the same prices.
The first one is done for you.

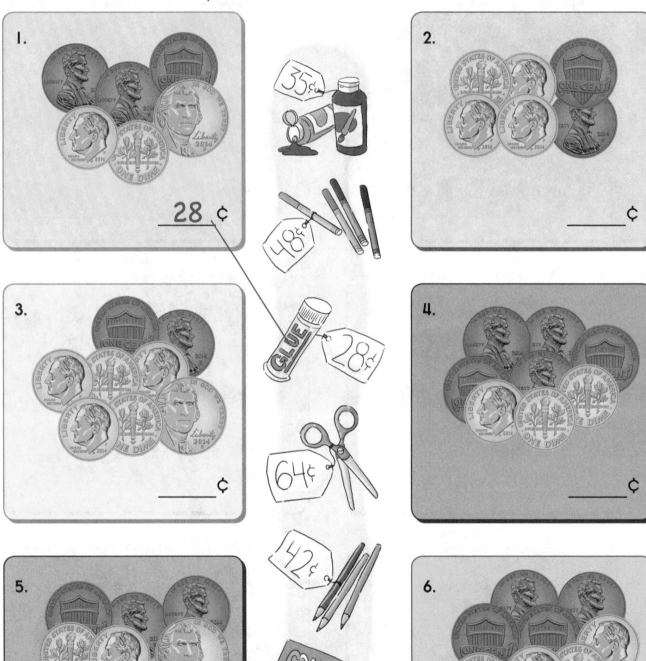

1. 28 ¢

2. _____ ¢

3. _____ ¢

4. _____ ¢

5. _____ ¢

6. _____ ¢

35¢

48¢

28¢

64¢

42¢

57¢

A clock has two hands.
The short hand shows the **hours**.
The long hand shows the **minutes**.

minute hand

hour hand

__2__ o'clock

__2__ : __00__

When the long hand points to the 12, we say, "o'clock."
To which hour does the short hand point?

Write the times.

1. _____ o'clock

_____ : _____

2. _____ o'clock

_____ : _____

3. _____ o'clock

_____ : _____

4. _____ o'clock

_____ : _____

5. _____ o'clock

_____ : _____

6. _____ o'clock

_____ : _____

When the minute hand points to the 6, it is half past the hour. The hour hand is halfway between the current and next hour numbers.

Half past __2__

__2__ : __30__

Write the times.

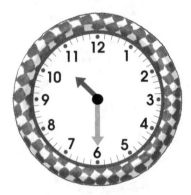

1. Half past _____

_____ : _____

2. Half past _____

_____ : _____

3. Half past _____

_____ : _____

4. Half past _____

_____ : _____

5. Half past _____

_____ : _____

6. Half past _____

_____ : _____

When the minute hand points to the 3, it is a quarter past the hour. The hour hand is a little past the hour.

Quarter past ___2___

___2___ : ___15___

Write the times.

1. Quarter past _____

_____ : _____

2. Quarter past _____

_____ : _____

3. Quarter past _____

_____ : _____

4. Quarter past _____

_____ : _____

5. Quarter past _____

_____ : _____

6. Quarter past _____

_____ : _____

TIME: QUARTER TO THE HOUR

When the minute hand points to the 9, it is a quarter to the next hour. The hour hand is closer to the next hour.

Quarter to ___3___

___2___ : __45__

Write the times.

1. Quarter to _____

_____ : _____

2. Quarter to _____

_____ : _____

3. Quarter to _____

_____ : _____

4. Quarter to _____

_____ : _____

5. Quarter to _____

_____ : _____

6. Quarter to _____

_____ : _____

EQUAL PARTS OF WHOLES

This shape has two equal parts.
Each part is $\frac{1}{2}$ or one-half of the whole.

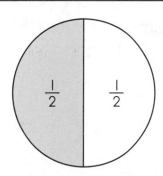

Find the shapes that show halves.
Write $\frac{1}{2}$ in each part.

1.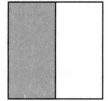

2.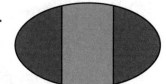

3.

4.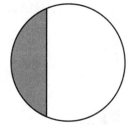

5.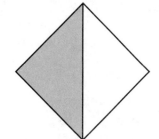

6.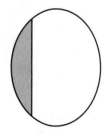

Color $\frac{1}{2}$ of each shape.

7.

8.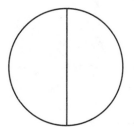

9.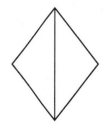

10.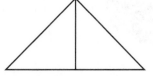

11.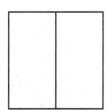

12.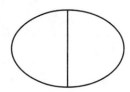

A **fraction** names a part of a whole.
The bottom of a fraction tells how many parts there are in all.

 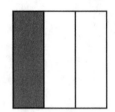 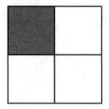

I of 2 equal parts is $\frac{1}{2}$. I of 3 equal parts is $\frac{1}{3}$. I of 4 equal parts is $\frac{1}{4}$.

Count the parts of the shapes. Write the numbers in the boxes to make fractions. The first one is done for you.

1. 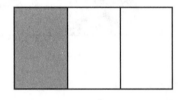 $\frac{1}{\boxed{3}}$

2. 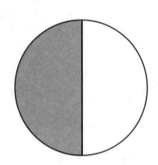 $\frac{1}{\boxed{}}$

3. 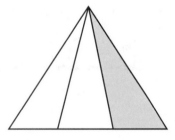 $\frac{1}{\boxed{}}$

4.  $\frac{1}{\boxed{}}$

5. 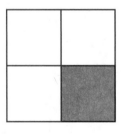 $\frac{1}{\boxed{}}$

6. 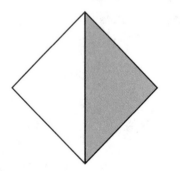 $\frac{1}{\boxed{}}$

HALVES, THIRDS, AND FOURTHS

A fraction tells how many parts of a whole are being used.
These fractions tell about the colored part of each shape.

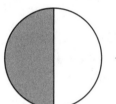 $\frac{1}{2}$

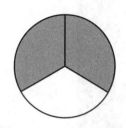 $\frac{2 \leftarrow \text{parts colored}}{3 \leftarrow \text{equal parts}}$

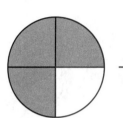 $\frac{3}{4}$

Write the fractions to tell about the colored parts of the shapes.
The first one is done for you.

1. 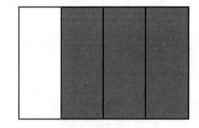 $\frac{\boxed{3}}{4}$

2. 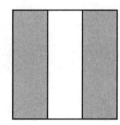 $\frac{2}{\boxed{}}$

3. 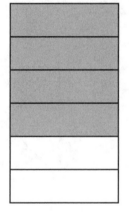 $\frac{\boxed{}}{\boxed{}}$

4. 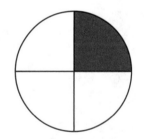 $\frac{\boxed{}}{\boxed{}}$

5. 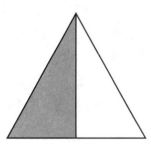 $\frac{\boxed{}}{\boxed{}}$

6. 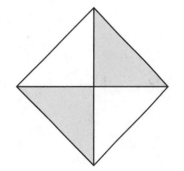 $\frac{\boxed{}}{\boxed{}}$

$\dfrac{3}{4}$ ←parts colored
←equal parts

Color the correct numbers of parts to show the fractions.

1. $\dfrac{2}{2}$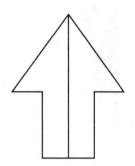

2. $\dfrac{2}{3}$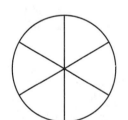

3. $\dfrac{5}{6}$

4. $\dfrac{2}{4}$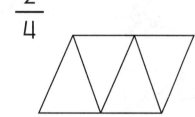

5. $\dfrac{4}{6}$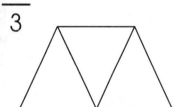

6. $\dfrac{3}{4}$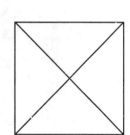

7. $\dfrac{5}{8}$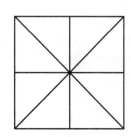

8. $\dfrac{1}{2}$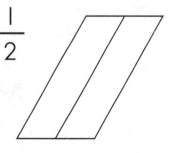

9. $\dfrac{3}{5}$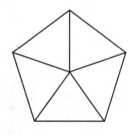

A **fraction** can also name a part of a group.

1 of 3 equal parts is $\frac{1}{3}$.

Circle the objects to show the fractions.

1. $\frac{1}{4}$
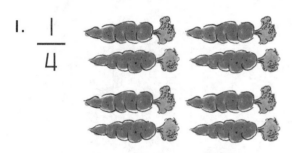

2. $\frac{1}{2}$

3. $\frac{1}{3}$

4. $\frac{1}{2}$

5. $\frac{1}{4}$

6. $\frac{1}{3}$

7. $\frac{1}{2}$

8. $\frac{1}{4}$

2 green mugs → $\frac{2}{3}$
3 mugs in all →

Write the fractions to tell about the colored parts of the groups.
The first one is done for you.

1. $\frac{1}{2}$

2. $\frac{2}{}$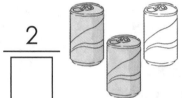

3.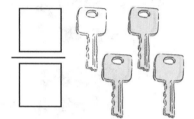

4.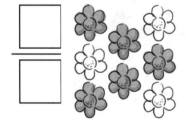

5.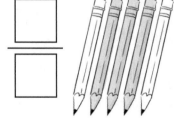

6.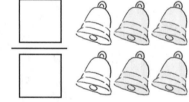

7.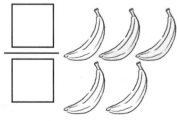

8.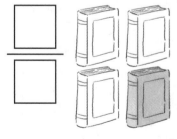

9.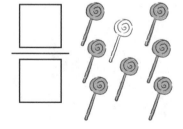

SHOWING FRACTIONS

$$\frac{2}{5}$$ ← 2 bones colored
← 5 bones in all

Color the objects to show the fractions.

1. $\frac{2}{3}$

2. $\frac{1}{2}$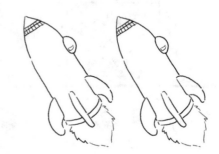

3. $\frac{3}{4}$

4. $\frac{4}{8}$

5. $\frac{2}{4}$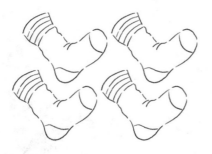

6. $\frac{3}{5}$

7. $\frac{7}{8}$

8. $\frac{5}{6}$

Number of Pets

	1	2	3	4	5	6
Carlos	🐶	🐶				
Ann	🐦	🐦	🐦			
Jamal	🦎					
Becky	🐟	🐟	🐟	🐟	🐟	🐟
Suri	🐱					
Phil	🐭	🐭	🐭			

0   1   2   3   4   5   6

Use the picture graph to answer the questions.
How many pets does each child have?

1. Carlos _____   2. Becky _____   3. Ann _____

4. Suri _____   5. Jamal _____   6. Phil _____

7. How many pets do Carlos and Phil have in all?

_____ ☐ _____ = _____

8. Becky has more pets than Ann.
How many more pets does Becky have?

_____ ☐ _____ = _____

PICTURE GRAPHS

Number of Golf Balls Hit

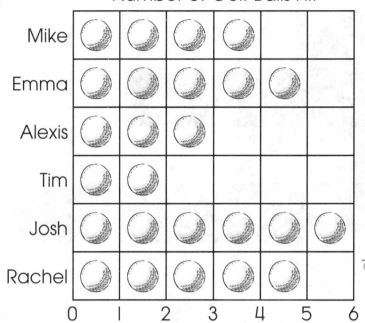

Use the picture graph to answer the questions.

1. How many golf balls did Mike hit? _____

2. How many golf balls did Emma hit? _____

3. How many golf balls did Alexis hit? _____

4. How many golf balls did Tim hit? _____

5. How many golf balls did Josh hit? _____

6. How many golf balls did Rachel hit? _____

7. How many golf balls did Alexis and Emma hit altogether?

_____ ☐ _____ = _____

8. Josh hit more golf balls than Mike.
   How many more golf balls did Josh hit?

_____ ☐ _____ = _____

Number of Books Read

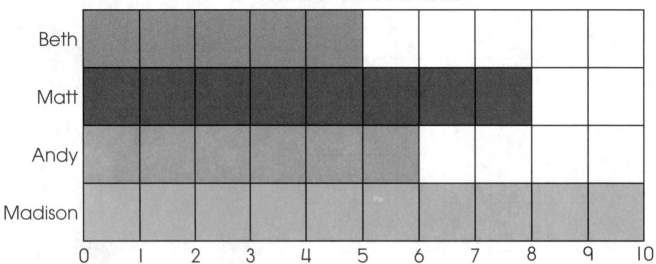

| | 0 | 1 | 2 | 3 | 4 | 5 | 6 | 7 | 8 | 9 | 10 |

Beth, Matt, Andy, Madison

Use the bar graph to answer the questions.

1. How many books did Beth read? _____

2. How many books did Andy read? _____

3. How many books did Andy and Matt read in all?

   _____ ☐ _____ = _____

4. How many books did Madison and Matt read altogether?

   _____ ☐ _____ = _____

5. Madison read more books than Andy. How many more books did Madison read?

   _____ ☐ _____ = _____

6. How many books did Andy and Beth read in all?

   _____ ☐ _____ = _____

BAR GRAPHS

Number of Tickets

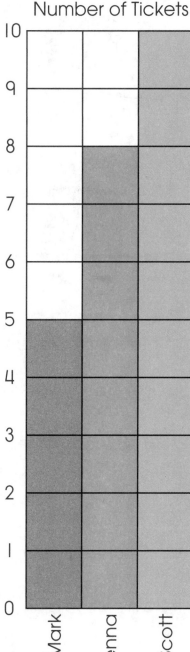

Use the bar graph to answer the questions.

1. How many tickets does Mark have? _____

2. How many tickets does Scott have? _____

3. How many tickets does Jenna have? _____

4. Jenna has more tickets than Mark.
   How many more tickets does Jenna have?

   _____ □ _____ = _____

5. Scott has more tickets than Mark. How
   many more tickets does Scott have?

   _____ □ _____ = _____

6. How many tickets do Mark and Jenna
   have altogether?

   _____ □ _____ = _____

Favorite Zoo Animals

monkey	//// //// ///
lion	//// ////
penguin	//// //// //
polar bear	//// /
alligator	////

/ = 1 vote

//// = 5 votes

Use the tally table to solve the problems.

1. How many votes did the alligator get? _____

2. How many votes did the monkey get? _____

3. How many votes did the penguin get? _____

4. Which zoo animal got the most votes? _____

5. Which zoo animal got the fewest votes? _____

6. The lion got more votes than the polar bear. How many more votes did the lion get?

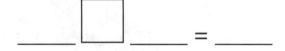

7. How many votes did the monkey and the alligator get in all?

Use the calendar to solve the problems.

April						
Sunday	**Monday**	**Tuesday**	**Wednesday**	**Thursday**	**Friday**	**Saturday**
			1		3	4
5		7		9		11
12	13		15		17	
19		21		23		25
	27		29			

1. Write the missing numbers in the calendar.

2. Which day comes after Thursday? _____

3. Which day comes before Sunday? _____

4. What day of the week is April 12? _____

5. What is the date of the first Wednesday? _____

6. What is the date of the second Monday? _____

7. How many days are in one week? _____

8. How many days are in two weeks? _____ ☐ _____ = _____

9. How many days are in April? _____

ADDING TENS AND ONES

Follow these steps to add tens and ones:

1. Add the ones.
2. Add the tens.

Step 1

```
 tens ones
   2  4
 + 1  3
 _____
      7
```

Step 2

```
 tens ones
   2  4
 + 1  3
 _____
   3  7
```

Add to find the sums.

1.
```
  27
+ 60
____
```

2.
```
  25
+  3
____
```

3.
```
  91
+  6
____
```

4.
```
  45
+ 14
____
```

5.
```
  44
+ 34
____
```

6.
```
  52
+  6
____
```

7.
```
  60
+  8
____
```

8.
```
  83
+  6
____
```

9.
```
  72
+  1
____
```

10.
```
  63
+  5
____
```

11.
```
  13
+  4
____
```

12.
```
  25
+ 22
____
```

Follow these steps to subtract tens and ones:

1. Subtract the ones.
2. Subtract the tens.

Step 1

```
tens ones
 5  7
- 1  2
-----
    5
```

Step 2

```
tens ones
 5  7
- 1  2
-----
 4  5
```

Subtract to find the differences.

1. $\begin{array}{r} 38 \\ -\ 6 \\ \hline \end{array}$

2. $\begin{array}{r} 24 \\ -\ 3 \\ \hline \end{array}$

3. $\begin{array}{r} 57 \\ -\ 5 \\ \hline \end{array}$

4. $\begin{array}{r} 98 \\ -\ 6 \\ \hline \end{array}$

5. $\begin{array}{r} 25 \\ -\ 2 \\ \hline \end{array}$

6. $\begin{array}{r} 49 \\ -\ 7 \\ \hline \end{array}$

7. $\begin{array}{r} 47 \\ -\ 15 \\ \hline \end{array}$

8. $\begin{array}{r} 65 \\ -\ 22 \\ \hline \end{array}$

9. $\begin{array}{r} 86 \\ -\ 26 \\ \hline \end{array}$

10. $\begin{array}{r} 96 \\ -\ 23 \\ \hline \end{array}$

11. $\begin{array}{r} 78 \\ -\ 54 \\ \hline \end{array}$

12. $\begin{array}{r} 48 \\ -\ 34 \\ \hline \end{array}$

RACE TO THE MONKEYS

Take turns giving the answer to every other problem.
The player who has the most correct answers wins.

3 tens + 7 ones = _____

Start

$$\begin{array}{r} 3 \\ + 4 \\ \hline \end{array}$$

$$\begin{array}{r} 6 \\ - 3 \\ \hline \end{array}$$

$$\begin{array}{r} 8 \\ + 2 \\ \hline \end{array}$$

$$\begin{array}{r} 7 \\ - 5 \\ \hline \end{array}$$

$$\begin{array}{r} 9 \\ + 3 \\ \hline \end{array}$$

$$\begin{array}{r} 12 \\ - 4 \\ \hline \end{array}$$

_____ 85 _____

$$\begin{array}{r} 10 \\ + 6 \\ \hline \end{array}$$

$$\begin{array}{r} 9 \\ - \square \\ \hline 6 \end{array}$$

$$\begin{array}{r} 8 \\ + 4 \\ \hline \end{array}$$

$$\begin{array}{r} 12 \\ - 3 \\ \hline \end{array}$$

$$\begin{array}{r} 9 \\ + 2 \\ \hline \end{array}$$

$$\begin{array}{r} 6 \\ + \square \\ \hline 12 \end{array}$$

$$\begin{array}{r} 12 \\ - 7 \\ \hline \end{array}$$

$$\begin{array}{r} 11 \\ + 5 \\ \hline \end{array}$$

$$\begin{array}{r} 8 \\ + 3 \\ \hline \end{array}$$

$$\begin{array}{r} 12 \\ - \square \\ \hline 8 \end{array}$$

$$\begin{array}{r} 10 \\ - 3 \\ \hline \end{array}$$

$$\begin{array}{r} 10 \\ + 8 \\ \hline \end{array}$$

$$\begin{array}{r} 15 \\ - \square \\ \hline 10 \end{array}$$

$$\begin{array}{r} 12 \\ - 5 \\ \hline \end{array}$$

$$\begin{array}{r} 13 \\ - \square \\ \hline 7 \end{array}$$

$$\begin{array}{r} 11 \\ + 7 \\ \hline \end{array}$$

$$\begin{array}{r} 20 \\ + 10 \\ \hline \end{array}$$

6 tens + 4 ones = _____

$$\begin{array}{r} 18 \\ + 1 \\ \hline \end{array}$$

$$\begin{array}{r} 11 \\ - \square \\ \hline 7 \end{array}$$

$$\begin{array}{r} 6 \\ + \square \\ \hline 14 \end{array}$$

$$\begin{array}{r} 10 \\ + \square \\ \hline 12 \end{array}$$

$$\begin{array}{r} 12 \\ - \square \\ \hline 5 \end{array}$$

Finish

ANSWER KEY

Page 2
1. dog
2. cat
3. fish
4. bird

Page 3
1. fan, lamp
2. apple, bat
3. ant, ham
4. map, cat

Page 4
1. egg, tent
2. web, bed
3. jet, desk
4. ten, nest

Page 5
1. bib, wig
2. ship, six
3. fish, mittens
4. pig, pin

Page 6
1. fox, top
2. doll, lock
3. box, rocket
4. sock, mop

Page 7
1. sun, rug
2. cup, bus
3. gum, hug
4. duck, tub

Page 8

Page 9
1. ten 2. cat 3. pig
4. bus 5. doll 6. fan
7. fish 8. nest 9. duck

Page 10
1. snail
2. cake
3. rain
4. day
5. gray, gate

Page 11
1. three
2. tree
3. sheep
4. leaf
5. he, me

Page 12
1. bike
2. nine
3. fly
4. right
5. tight, tie

Page 13
1. goat
2. rope
3. boat
4. rose
5. nose, note

Page 14
1. tube
2. glue
3. huge
4. cute
5. few, new

Page 15

Page 16

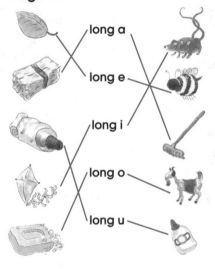

long a
long e
long i
long o
long u

Page 17

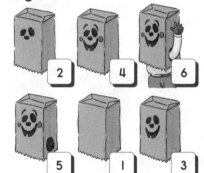

Page 18
1. fourth
2. second
3. first
4. third
5. fifth

Page 19

Living	Non-living
dog	ball
bird	top
goat	doll

Page 20

Page 21

Page 22
1. yes
2. no
3. yes
4. yes
5. no
6. no

Page 23

1. 3 2 1
2. 1 3 2

Page 24

3	FERRIS WHEEL
5	ROLLER COASTER
1	BUMPER CARS
4	LOG RIDE
2	CAROUSEL
6	WAVE POOL

Favorite rides will vary.

Page 25

ANSWER KEY

Page 26
1. new
2. closed
3. hot
4. open
5. old
6. cold

Page 27

Page 28
 Zeke
 Jill
Pedro
 Adam
Anna

Page 29
 Rachel
 Eddie
 Sue
Beth
Peter

Page 30

1.
2.
3.
4.

Page 31
Liz   Henry
Chan   Stacy

Page 32

	milk	juice	fruit	salad	taco	sandwich
Dad	✓		✓		✓	
Jake		✓	✓		✓	
Mom		✓	✓	✓		
Ashley		✓	✓			✓

Jake   Ashley

Mom   Dad

Page 33
1. our dog is hungry.
2. dad brings food.
3. skip eats quickly.
4. food goes on the floor.
5. dogs are messy.
6. now I need to clean up.
7. Answers will vary.

Page 34
1. is Mother home?
2. where did she go?
3. when will she be back?
4. who baked the cookies?
5. they are good.
6. may I have another one?
7. Answers will vary.

Page 35
1. Dad
2. farmer
3. cows
4. dog
5. chicken

Page 36

Places	Things
zoo	book
house	pizza
town	bike

Answers will vary–make sure words name a place and a thing.

Page 37
1. dogs
2. spots
3. ears
4. cats
5. bones

Page 38
1. play
2. hits
3. flies
4. runs
5. catch

Page 39
1. plants
2. grows
3. pulls
4. waters
5. eats

Page 40
1. hot
2. loud
3. cold
4. soft
5. wet

Page 41
1. big
2. three
3. striped
4. black
5. little
6. four
7. Answers will vary–make sure describing word is underlined.

Page 42
1. don't
2. aren't
3. haven't
4. Let's
5. won't

Page 43
1. 4   2. 2
3. 4   4. 4
5. 5   6. 3

Page 44
1. 2   2. 2
3. 3   4. 1
5. 1   6. 2

Page 45
1. 5   2. 5   3. 8
4. 7   5. 8   6. 7
7. 7   8. 8   9. 8
10. 5   11. 4   12. 4

Page 46
1. 1   2. 4   3. 2
4. 1   5. 4   6. 2
7. 7   8. 1   9. 2
10. 0   11. 6   12. 4

Page 47
1. 7   2. 8   3. 8   4. 6
5. 7   6. 8   7. 7   8. 6
9. 1   10. 0   11. 6   12. 2
13. 3   14. 2   15. 2   16. 3

Page 48
1. 12   2. 11   3. 12
4. 10   5. 12   6. 12
7. 9   8. 12   9. 10   10. 9
11. 10 12. 11 13. 11 14. 12

Page 49
1. 7   2. 7   3. 9
4. 5   5. 6   6. 4
7. 8   8. 5   9. 4   10. 4
11. 8   12. 6   13. 6   14. 9

Page 50
1. 9	**2.** 10	**3.** 8	**4.** 11
5. 12	**6.** 11	**7.** 7	**8.** 8
9. 12	**10.** 9	**11.** 10	**12.** 12
13. 8	**14.** 9	**15.** 10	**16.** 11

Page 51
1. 7	**2.** 5	**3.** 5	**4.** 4
5. 3	**6.** 5	**7.** 8	**8.** 3
9. 3	**10.** 1	**11.** 7	**12.** 6
13. 4	**14.** 9	**15.** 1	**16.** 5

Page 52
1. 5	**2.** 8	**3.** 11	**4.** 6
5. 9	**6.** 9	**7.** 10	**8.** 12
9. 6	**10.** 3	**11.** 10	**12.** 5
13. 10	**14.** 5	**15.** 12	**16.** 7

Page 53
1. −	**2.** −	**3.** +
4. −	**5.** +	**6.** −
7. −	**8.** +	**9.** +
10. −	**11.** +	**12.** −
13. +	**14.** −	**15.** +

Page 54

10	0	8	12	4	9
− 2	+ 8	+ 1	− 7	+ 1	− 3
8	8	9	5	5	6
+ 4	− 3	+ 2	+ 6	− 0	+ 5
12	5	11	11	5	11
− 5	+ 7	− 4	− 1	+ 6	− 3
=	=	=	=	=	=
7	12	7	10	11	8

Page 55
1. (7 + 3) / 8 + 1 / (5 + 5) / (6 + 4)
2. (9 + 2) / (6 + 5) / 8 + 4 / (3 + 8)
3. (4 + 8) / (9 + 3) / (5 + 7) / (6 + 6)

4. 5 + 7 / (8 + 5) / (10 + 3) / (9 + 4)
5. (4 + 10) / (7 + 7) / (6 + 8) / (5 + 9)
6. (10 + 5) / 11 + 3 / (8 + 7) / (9 + 6)

7. (8 + 8) / 7 + 9 / (6 + 10) / 12 + 5
8. (6 + 11) / (10 + 7) / (9 + 8) / 7 + 9
9. (12 + 6) / (7 + 11) / (10 + 8) / (9 + 9)

Page 56
1. (12 − 2) / 15 − 6 / (14 − 4) / (13 − 3)
2. (13 − 2) / (11 − 0) / (12 − 1) / (15 − 4)
3. (14 − 2) / (16 − 4) / 17 − 4 / (15 − 3)

4. (17 − 4) / (15 − 2) / (14 − 1) / 18 − 4
5. 12 − 2 / (18 − 4) / (16 − 2) / (17 − 3)
6. (18 − 3) / (16 − 1) / (17 − 2) / 12 − 3

7. (16 − 0) / 15 − 1 / (18 − 2) / (17 − 1)
8. 15 − 2 / (18 − 1) / 16 − 1 / (17 − 0)
9. 17 − 1 / (18 − 0) / 16 − 2 / 15 − 3

Page 57
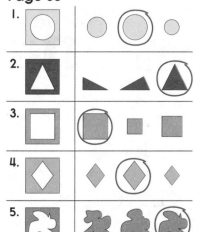

8	16	4	9	5	17
+ 4	− 8	+ 10	+ 8	+ 4	− 5
12	8	14	17	9	12
+ 6	− 7	+ 2	− 5	+ 6	− 1
18	1	16	12	15	11
− 1	+ 3	− 3	+ 6	− 7	+ 5
=	=	=	=	=	=
17	4	13	18	8	16

Page 58
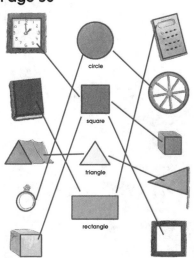

Page 59
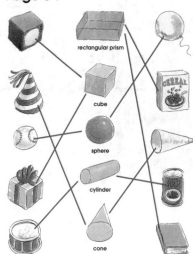

Page 60

Page 61
1. 1 ten 10	**2.** 2 tens 20
3. 3 tens 30	**4.** 4 tens 40
5. 5 tens 50	**6.** 6 tens 60
7. 7 tens 70	**8.** 8 tens 80
9. 9 tens 90	

10. 10, 20, 30, 40, 50, 60, 70, 80, 90, 100
11. 10, 20, 30, 40, 50, 60, 70, 80, 90, 100

Page 62
1. 1 ten   4 ones
14
2. 2 tens   2 ones
22
3. 3 tens   4 ones
34
4. 2 tens   0 ones
20
5. 1 ten   7 ones
17
6. 1 ten   8 ones
18

Page 63
	tens	ones		tens	ones
1.	6	5	2.	2	8
3.	5	4	4.	6	6
5.	4	0	6.	3	4
7.	8	1	8.	1	7
9.	3	0	10.	7	1
11.	1	9	12.	2	5

Page 64
1. 31 2. 35 3. 50
4. 43 5. 15 6. 31
7. 18 8. 21 9. 23
10. 44 11. 13 12. 18
13. 78 14. 25 15. 23
16. 20 17. 59 18. 48

Page 65
1. 44 2. 26 3. 23 4. 32
5. 80 6. 29 7. 17 8. 66
9. 92 10. 54 11. 41
12. 25 13. 18 14. 37
15. 7 16. 48 17. 26 18. 20
19. 93 20. 51 21. 75 22. 12

Page 66
1. 6¢
2. 30¢
3. 80¢

Page 67
1. 10¢, 20¢, 25¢, 30¢, 31¢, 32¢, 33¢; 33¢
2. 10¢, 15¢, 20¢, 21¢, 22¢, 23¢, 24¢; 24¢
3. 10¢, 20¢, 30¢, 35¢, 40¢, 41¢, 42¢; 42¢
4. 10¢, 20¢, 30¢, 35¢, 40¢, 45¢, 46¢; 46¢

Page 68
1. 10¢, 20¢, 25¢, 26¢, 27¢, 28¢; 28¢
2. 10¢, 20¢, 25¢, 30¢, 31¢, 32¢; 32¢
3. 5¢, 10¢, 15¢, 20¢, 25¢, 26¢; 26¢
4. 5¢, 10¢, 11¢, 12¢, 13¢, 14¢; 14¢
5. 10¢, 15¢, 20¢, 21¢, 22¢, 23¢; 23¢

Page 69
1. 15¢ 2. 17¢
3. 30¢ 4. 23¢
5. 16¢ 6. 40¢

Page 70
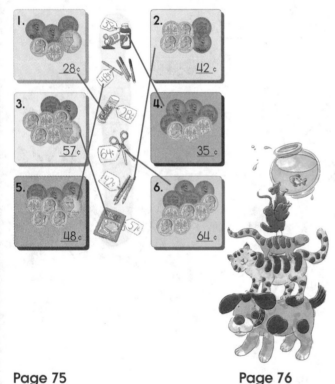

Page 71
1. 7 o'clock
7:00
2. 1 o'clock
1:00
3. 11 o'clock
11:00
4. 3 o'clock
3:00
5. 5 o'clock
5:00
6. 12 o'clock
12:00

Page 72
1. Half past 10
10:30
2. Half past 4
4:30
3. Half past 9
9:30
4. Half past 3
3:30
5. Half past 8
8:30
6. Half past 6
6:30

Page 73
1. Quarter past 6
6:15
2. Quarter past 8
8:15
3. Quarter past 1
1:15
4. Quarter past 12
12:15
5. Quarter past 10
10:15
6. Quarter past 7
7:15

Page 74
1. Quarter to 4
3:45
2. Quarter to 9
8:45
3. Quarter to 1
12:45
4. Quarter to 7
6:45
5. Quarter to 2
1:45
6. Quarter to 10
9:45

Page 75
1. $\frac{1}{2}$ $\frac{1}{2}$ 2. 3. $\frac{1}{2}$ $\frac{1}{2}$
4. 5. $\frac{1}{2}$ $\frac{1}{2}$ 6.
7. 8. 9.
10. 11. 12.

Section colored can vary.

Page 76
1. $\frac{1}{3}$ 2. $\frac{1}{2}$
3. $\frac{1}{3}$ 4. $\frac{1}{4}$
5. $\frac{1}{4}$ 6. $\frac{1}{2}$

Page 77
1. $\frac{3}{4}$ 2. $\frac{2}{3}$
3. $\frac{4}{6}$ 4. $\frac{1}{4}$
5. $\frac{1}{2}$ 6. $\frac{2}{4}$

Page 78

1. $\frac{2}{2}$
2. $\frac{2}{3}$
3. $\frac{5}{6}$

4. $\frac{2}{4}$
5. $\frac{4}{6}$
6. $\frac{3}{4}$

7. $\frac{5}{8}$
8. $\frac{1}{2}$
9. $\frac{3}{5}$

Sections colored can vary.

Page 79

1. $\frac{1}{4}$
2. $\frac{1}{2}$

3. $\frac{1}{3}$
4. $\frac{1}{2}$

5. $\frac{1}{4}$
6. $\frac{1}{3}$

7. $\frac{1}{2}$
8. $\frac{1}{4}$

Objects circled can vary.

Page 80

1. $\frac{1}{2}$
2. $\frac{2}{3}$
3. $\frac{3}{4}$

4. $\frac{5}{8}$
5. $\frac{3}{5}$
6. $\frac{4}{6}$

7. $\frac{2}{5}$
8. $\frac{1}{4}$
9. $\frac{7}{8}$

Page 81

1. $\frac{2}{3}$
2. $\frac{1}{2}$

3. $\frac{3}{4}$
4. $\frac{4}{8}$

5. $\frac{2}{4}$
6. $\frac{3}{5}$

7. $\frac{7}{8}$
8. $\frac{5}{6}$

Objects colored can vary.

Page 82

1. 2   2. 6   3. 3
4. 1   5. 1   6. 3
7. 2 + 3 = 5
8. 6 − 3 = 3

Page 83

1. 4
2. 5
3. 3
4. 2
5. 6
6. 5
7. 3 + 5 = 8
8. 6 − 4 = 2

Page 84

1. 5
2. 6
3. 6 + 8 = 14
4. 10 + 8 = 18
5. 10 − 6 = 4
6. 6 + 5 = 11

Page 85

1. 5
2. 10
3. 8
4. 8 − 5 = 3
5. 10 − 5 = 5
6. 5 + 8 = 13

Page 86

1. 4
2. 13
3. 12
4. monkey
5. alligator
6. 10 − 6 = 4
7. 13 + 4 = 17

Page 87

1.

April						
Sunday	Monday	Tuesday	Wednesday	Thursday	Friday	Saturday
			1	2	3	4
5	6	7	8	9	10	11
12	13	14	15	16	17	18
19	20	21	22	23	24	25
26	27	28	29	30		

2. Friday
3. Saturday
4. Sunday
5. April 1
6. April 13
7. 7
8. 7 + 7 = 14
9. 30

Page 88

1. 87   2. 28   3. 97   4. 59
5. 78   6. 58   7. 68   8. 89
9. 73   10. 68   11. 17   12. 47

Page 89

1. 32   2. 21   3. 52   4. 92
5. 23   6. 42   7. 32   8. 43
9. 60   10. 73   11. 24   12. 14

Page 90

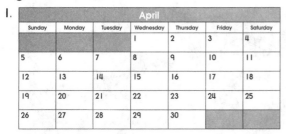

3 tens + 7 ones = 37

Start

$\begin{array}{r} 3 \\ + 4 \\ \hline 7 \end{array}$

$\begin{array}{r} 6 \\ - 3 \\ \hline 3 \end{array}$

$\begin{array}{r} 8 \\ + 2 \\ \hline 10 \end{array}$

$\begin{array}{r} 7 \\ - 5 \\ \hline 2 \end{array}$

$\begin{array}{r} 9 \\ + 3 \\ \hline 12 \end{array}$

$\begin{array}{r} 12 \\ - 4 \\ \hline 8 \end{array}$

84 85 86

$\begin{array}{r} 10 \\ + 6 \\ \hline 16 \end{array}$ $\begin{array}{r} 12 \\ - 7 \\ \hline 5 \end{array}$ $\begin{array}{r} 11 \\ + 5 \\ \hline 16 \end{array}$

$\begin{array}{r} 9 \\ - 3 \\ \hline 6 \end{array}$

$\begin{array}{r} 8 \\ + 4 \\ \hline 12 \end{array}$

$\begin{array}{r} 12 \\ - 3 \\ \hline 9 \end{array}$

$\begin{array}{r} 9 \\ + 2 \\ \hline 11 \end{array}$

$\begin{array}{r} 6 \\ + 6 \\ \hline 12 \end{array}$

$\begin{array}{r} 8 \\ + 3 \\ \hline 11 \end{array}$

$\begin{array}{r} 12 \\ - 4 \\ \hline 8 \end{array}$

$\begin{array}{r} 10 \\ - 3 \\ \hline 7 \end{array}$

6 tens + 4 ones = 64

$\begin{array}{r} 10 \\ + 8 \\ \hline 18 \end{array}$

$\begin{array}{r} 15 \\ - 5 \\ \hline 10 \end{array}$

$\begin{array}{r} 12 \\ - 5 \\ \hline 7 \end{array}$

$\begin{array}{r} 13 \\ - 6 \\ \hline 7 \end{array}$

$\begin{array}{r} 11 \\ + 7 \\ \hline 18 \end{array}$

$\begin{array}{r} 20 \\ + 10 \\ \hline 30 \end{array}$

$\begin{array}{r} 18 \\ + 1 \\ \hline 19 \end{array}$

$\begin{array}{r} 11 \\ - 4 \\ \hline 7 \end{array}$

$\begin{array}{r} 6 \\ + 8 \\ \hline 14 \end{array}$

$\begin{array}{r} 10 \\ + 2 \\ \hline 12 \end{array}$

$\begin{array}{r} 12 \\ - 7 \\ \hline 5 \end{array}$

Finish

AWARD

YIPPEE!

Great Job!

_____

Name

finished First Grade Basics
from School Zone Publishing Company.